Monetising And Empowering The Nigerian Driver

Jack's Curated Business Idea

By Jack Lookman

Monetising And Empowering The Nigerian Driver

Jack's Curated Business Idea

Copyright © 2023 Jack Lookman Limited

All rights reserved.
No portion of this book may be reproduced in whole or in part, in any form or by any means, electronic or mechanical including photocopying, recording, or by any information storage and retrieval system, without the consent and written permission from the author.

A. PREAMBLE

As a trained Engineer, I learnt to find solutions to problems.

Sometimes, I envisage challenges, and the opportunities they present.

This content is an attempt at finding a cost effective solution to a problem which is commonly disregarded.

I've married problem solving, creative, social Engineering, Content Creation and Entrepreneurial skills; with the hope of being part of the value chain in solving this problem.

Have a great read.

Ire awawa ri o. (May you find the blessings that you desire)

Ire kabiti (I wish you loads of blessings)

Olayinka Carew aka Jack Lookman

A Jack Lookman Limited 2023 product

jacklookman@yahoo.co.uk

jacksempowerment.com.   jacklookman.co.uk.   jaaloo.com

B. ACKNOWLEDGEMENT

I continue to be grateful to my Creator and Sustainer, for known and unknown favours and blessings.

I appreciate my parents, for being the vehicle of success.

I was fortified with spiritual and academic knowledge and practices; as well as great life skills.

Contributions of John Tosin Adekunle are appreciated.

Mr Edo, Ire o (I wish you blessings).

Taiwo and Owolabi are appreciated; you continue your good deeds very quietly.

Brother Roland Owolabi, you are appreciated.

Sister Seyi Sikirat, thank you.

Chinedu China, I appreciate you. Are you Chinese or Nigerian?

My beautiful Tolu Mayowa Tobi you are very much appreciated.

To all those who've added value to me, I say, thank you.

To my Creator and Sustainer: Alhamdu lillahi rabbi alAAalameena.

jacksempowerment.com.   jacklookman.co.uk.   jaaloo.com

C. DEDICATION

This piece of work is dedicated to all my family members.

My Late Dad

My Mum

My Siblings

My Children

May Allah grant us goodness in this world and the hereafter and protect us from the torment of hell fire. Ameen.

jacksempowerment.com.   jacklookman.co.uk.   jaaloo.com

Dedication

This piece of work is dedicated to my family mainly:

My wife

TAVSHIRZ

My Mother

Mrs. Jajja mariam gindesasio, Late david, and the whole Jajja Dickson family bank J.D BANK round roll the ages.

Monetising And Empowering The Nigerian Driver
1

Jack's Curated Business Idea
1

A. PREAMBLE
3

MONETISING AND EMPOWERING THE NIGERIAN DRIVER
10

1. Introduction
10

2. Some Benefits of the Idea
10

3. Some Considerations for the Business Plan
11

4. Some Challenges that may be Faced
11

5. Pricing Considerations
11

6. Some Curriculum that could be Explored
12

7. Format of Digital Content
15

8. What are the Opportunities Presented?
15

9. Is there a need for Research and Development?
16

10. What is the Value Proposition?
16

11. What Problem are you Solving?
17

12. A Perception of the Nigerian driver
18

13. Inspiration for this Idea
19

14. What's the Unique Selling Point?
19

15. Here are Some things to Ponder…
19

16. How Could this Idea Impact Others?
20

17. Could Some of the Content be Cross Sold?
20

18. Here Are Some Monetisation Options
21

19. What's the Marketing Plan?
21

20. What's the Pricing Plan?
22

21. What are Costing Considerations?
23

22. What are diversification options for this product?
23

23. Is There a Need to Collaborate?
24

24. Could I Monetize for a Lifetime?
24

25. Is this Idea only for Nigeria?
24

26. What Platforms Could be Used?
24

27. Could the Product be Gifted?
25

28. What are potential threats?
25

29. On What Platforms Could the Product/s be Sold?
26

30. What will be the Mode of Payment?
26

31. Suggested Questionnaire for the Driver
27

32. In What Format will the Product Be?
27

33. What will be the User Interface?
28

34. On which Gadgets Could the Content be Accessed?
28

35. Some Requirements for this Business are:
28

36. Some Required Skills:
29

37. Disclaimer
30

38. Conclusion
30

39. About Jack Lookman
31

40. OTHER PUBLICATIONS BY Jack Lookman Limited
32

41. Some Useful Links
34

MONETISING AND EMPOWERING THE NIGERIAN DRIVER

1. Introduction

Hello! Welcome to another presentation in our series, Jack's Curated Business Ideas. This is Olayinka Carew aka Jack Lookman. I shall explore an uncommon idea of monetising and empowering the Nigerian Driver. This idea could however be applied to other demographics and niches. You could find much more content on our different platforms. This content could be a great resource for Content Creators, Entrepreneurs, Entrepreneurial minds, Drivers, Educators, Investors, Collaborators, those seeking full time or side hustles, and similar others. We do collaborations, as well as mentoring. Please contact us at jacklookman@yahoo.co.uk

Let's dive into the topic.

2. Some Benefits of the Idea

- Added value to drivers.
- Optimising the potential of drivers.
- Added value to society.
- Wealth creation opportunities.
- Job creation opportunities for Content Creators.
- Renewed opportunities for drivers.

jacksempowerment.com.   jacklookman.co.uk.   jaaloo.com

3. Some Considerations for the Business Plan

- Research and Development
- Finance
- Collaboration
- Profit Sharing Formula
- Monetisation plan
- Customer retention
- Automation
- Marketing plan

4. Some Challenges that may be Faced

- Non acceptance in changing the status quo
- Resistance to change
- Negative feedback
- Financial constraints along the way
- Having the will power to see the idea through

jacksempowerment.com.   jacklookman.co.uk.   jaaloo.com

5. Pricing Considerations

- Affordability

- Customer longevity
- Competition
- Value
- Profit
- Customer potential
- Sales funnel

6. Some Curriculum that could be Explored

- Customer services
- Entrepreneurship
- Interpersonal skills
- Mindset
- Risk management
- Learning and sharing best practice
- Skill enhancement
- Investment opportunities
- Business diversification
- Basic Research
- How to invest wisely
- Health and well being
- Investments
- Cash flow
- Industry best practice

- Preparing for grey years
- Family matters
- Potential pitfalls
- Spirituality
- Benefits of team work
- Opportunities in the driving industry
- Legalities
- Effective communication
- Optimising the internet
- Money management
- People management
- Leveraging strengths
- Optimising resources
- Overcoming weaknesses
- Time management
- Skills audit
- Interest audit
- Resource management
- Importance of Mentoring And Coaching
- Importance of integrity
- Importance of reliability
- Importance of holidays
- Value chain

- Building lifetime clients
- Safety
- Care of vehicle
- Work-life-balance
- Asset management
- Vehicle maintenance
- Business collaboration
- Business funding
- Passive income
- Time management
- Working smart
- Effectively leveraging resources
- Legalities
- Marketing plan
- Monetisation plan
- How to seek potential customers
- How to optimise potential customers
- Business requirements.
- Signposting
  - ☐ to mentors
  - ☐ coaches
  - ☐ content
  - ☐ opportunities

- ☐ courses
- ☐ seminars
- ☐ etc
■ Strategising for business
■ The client avatar etc

7. Format of Digital Content

- Concise audio/ video modules. It shall be easily understandable in language of the demographic
- Signposts to other content
- Signposts for mentoring
- Signposts for consultancy
- Signposts for collaborators
- Easy to navigate.
- Great user experience

8. What are the Opportunities Presented?

- The business opportunity
- Content creation opportunities
- Empowerment opportunities
- Fairer society
- Reduced crime

- Added value to drivers
- Job creation
- Wealth creation
- Added value to society
- Upsells, down-sells, cross sells
- Mentoring And Coaching opportunities

jacksempowerment.com.   jacklookman.co.uk.   jaaloo.com

9. Is there a need for Research and Development?

Yes, there is. Consider:

- Market research
- Product research
- Competitor research

10. What is the Value Proposition?

The value proposition is to empower that avatar by leveraging the internet and technology, and adding value to them, as well as to the society and by so-doing, the Content Creator could monetise. It ends up a win-win for one and all.

It will be digital courses and content, created for that demographic. It could also be applied to other demographics.

The courses shall be presented in little chunks, to make the learning process easy, effective and flexible.

The content could be accessible at any time or place, as long as there is an internet connection.

- Curated content shall be in languages of choice; e.g. pidgin English, Yoruba, Hausa, Ibo, etc
- Easy to understand
- Easy to navigate
- Affordable
- User friendly
- Different affordable price plans
- Great value
- Education for the less educated
- Creating learning opportunities for the less fortunate
- Create entrepreneurial opportunities, for Content Creators, Drivers, etc

  jacksempowerment.com. jacklookman.co.uk. jaaloo.com

11. What Problem are you Solving?

- The average Nigerian driver is very disadvantaged. He works very hard, probably with little to show for it. He's smart, but lacks opportunity. Mostly without an education due to financial or other constraints. He's resigned to being a driver probably as a last resort. The major problems being solved here are:

- Added value to drivers, who are mostly underpaid
- Job creation opportunities for Drivers, in and out of the profession
- Wealth creation opportunities for Drivers and non Drivers
- Added value to society, by educating that avatar
- Upsells, down-sells, cross sells for digital and other marketers
- Mentoring And Coaching opportunities for Content Creators and related others
- Creating opportunities for seasoned Drivers to share best practice
- Creating multiple opportunities for Drivers to leverage
- Improving the quality of life for Drivers and their dependants
- Creating a conducive and fairer society
- Educating the avatar at a very affordable price

12. A Perception of the Nigerian driver

- Hard working
- Financially deprived
- Educationally deprived
- Frustrated
- Abused
- Disenfranchised
- Hopeful
- Etc

13. Inspiration for this Idea

I had a chat with my dad's driver. This was as my dad's health deteriorated. I asked of his future plans and suggested a collaboration. He was very loyal to my dad. In fact, they had a father and son relationship. I was thinking ahead, as this was supposed to be part of my give back.

He thought of becoming self employed, by becoming a taxi Driver.

The limitations are however, that driving skills alone, are inadequate in running a thriving taxi business.

14. What's the Unique Selling Point?

The products are curated digital content in languages of choice, that could empower the avatar in attaining his full potential.

It brings learning and education to them at an affordable price. As well as in a user friendly way. They could access the content at their beck and call and consume what they need or choose.

jacksempowerment.com.   jacklookman.co.uk.   jaaloo.com

15. Here are Some things to Ponder…

- Do you prefer to continually give?
- Will you continually give fish, or teach how to fish?
- Are your monetary gifts more valuable than an education?
- Are they more valuable than empowerment?
- Are they more valuable than effectively signposting?

- Could the impact of your cash outweigh the empowerment for life?
- Could generations from that driver continually pray for you?
- Could society be enriched with your little gift?
- Could the content be given as a gift?

16. How Could this Idea Impact Others?

- Businesses could be created around the idea
- It could benefit drivers
- It could impact society positively
- It could reduce crime
- It could promote a fairer society
- It could create
    - [ ] jobs
    - [ ] wealth
    - [ ] open opportunities
    - [ ] the idea could be replicated in other niches and demographics
    - [ ] etc

jacksempowerment.com.   jacklookman.co.uk.   jaaloo.com

17. Could Some of the Content be Cross Sold?

Yes, they could.

- Some of the content modules may apply to different niches and demographics.
- It will be effective use of resources, to cross sell modules.
- You could 'copy and paste' such modules as necessary
- You could save resources, without depleting the value on offer
- You could also market and monetise modules independently

18. Here Are Some Monetisation Options

- Product sales
- Affiliate Marketing
- Adverts
- Upsells, down-sells, cross sells
- Collaborations
- License
- Public speaking
- Social media leverage etc

   jacksempowerment.com.   jacklookman.co.uk.   jaaloo.com

19. What's the Marketing Plan?

You could explore the undermentioned for marketing or advertising:
- Digital marketers.
- Affiliate Marketers

- Social Media Marketers
- Influencer marketers
- Branded products
- Radio marketing
- Google ads
- Television marketing
- Print media marketing
- Referrals
- Other traditional marketing
- Internet marketing
- Targeted events marketing
- Sponsored events
- Etc

20. What's the Pricing Plan?

You could have price plans to suit different wallet sizes.
- You could have monthly payers
- You could have quarterly or annual payers
- You could have a free product as a lead magnet (with adverts)
- You could sell the product/s as a license.
- You could sell it outright at a much higher price.

jacksempowerment.com.   jacklookman.co.uk.   jaaloo.com

21. What are Costing Considerations?

- Cost your time and other resources used.
- Consider competitors prices.
- Consider the value offer.
- Consider profit
- Consider demand and supply
- Consider affordability
- And any other considerations.

22. What are diversification options for this product?

- Individual digital products
- Combined digital products
- Collaborations with drivers and similar others
- Other digital products
- Explore different niches
- Upsells, down-sells, cross sells
- Affiliate Marketing
- Adverts

23. Is There a Need to Collaborate?

If you get the right collaborators:

- This could help lighten the load.
- You could learn and share from each other.
- You could share resources
- You could leverage each other.

24. Could I Monetize for a Lifetime?

Yes, potentially. You could even monetise in your grave. You could automate the process and literally get technology working for you.

25. Is this Idea only for Nigeria?

No, it's not. It could be applied to any country or any demographic and it could be sold globally.

jacksempowerment.com. jacklookman.co.uk. jaaloo.com

26. What Platforms Could be Used?

- Social media
- Membership sites
- Youtube
- Facebook

- Blog
- Podcast etc

27. Could the Product be Gifted?

Yes, it could;

- It could be a parting gift
- A gift while he's still an employee
- Or gift to those who may benefit
- It could be gifted through whatsapp other digital gadgets or platforms.
- It could be shared as a url link; or as a qr code to be scanned.

28. What are potential threats?

- Capacity to learn by the drivers
- Mindset issues from drivers and society
- Societal change of status quo
- Resistance to change
- Increased bargaining power of drivers
- Demand and supply issues for drivers
- Salaries for drivers could increase
- Intellectual theft of the idea or content

29. On What Platforms Could the Product/s be Sold?

- Affiliate Marketing platforms
- Digital platforms
- Membership sites
- Blogs
- Podcasts
- Websites
- Social media platforms
- Etc

30. What will be the Mode of Payment?

- Digital payments
- Debit or credit card
- Bank transfer
- Paypal
- Payoneer
- Etc

jacksempowerment.com.   jacklookman.co.uk.   jaaloo.com

31. Suggested Questionnaire for the Driver

- As part of the process, you may want to capture user data. This could include the undermentioned, in the questionnaire. That way, you could market other useful products and services to them sooner or later. The questionnaire shall capture:
- Skills
- Transferable skills
- Interests
- Vision
- Business interests
- Personality complements from family and friends
- Etc

32. In What Format will the Product Be?

- Text?
- Audio?
- Video?
- Etc?

jacksempowerment.com.   jacklookman.co.uk.   jaaloo.com

33. What will be the User Interface?

It could be:
- an app
- a website
- a blog
- a podcast
- a membership site
- social media
- etc

34. On which Gadgets Could the Content be Accessed?

- Smart phones
- Digital tablets
- Laptops
- Computers

35. Some Requirements for this Business are:

- Finance
- Equipment

- Skills
- Human resources
- Digital platforms
- Marketing platforms
- Content

36. Some Required Skills:

- Content creation
- Communication
- Language
- Basic information technology.
- Entrepreneurship/ business
- Marketing
- Research and Development
- Interpersonal
- Customer services
- Legal
- Knowledge of the industry
- Knowledge of local factors
- Knowledge of the trade

jacksempowerment.com. jacklookman.co.uk. jaaloo.com

37. Disclaimer

This content is intellectual, though it presents practical potentials. Yet, business success isn't guaranteed. You are expected to leverage the idea and modify it to your business needs and hopefully, business and financial success shall be attained.

38. Conclusion

As you may perceive, this is indeed a Curated Business Idea. It's not the usual cut and paste content. It's an idea with potential of a lot of empowerment for both the user and the entrepreneur.

It could actually be a 'blue ocean' with little competitors. You could therefore enjoy a monopoly.

I hope that you got value. If so, please consider spreading the word. You could access more content on our other platforms.

Search for Jack Lookman on the internet. We have content in text, audio and video formats. We also offer mentoring and collaborative services. Please contact us at jacklookman@yahoo.co.uk with a suitable subject heading, if interested.

This is Olayinka Carew aka Jack Lookman signing off

Ire o (I wish you blessings)

Ire kabiti (I wish you loads of blessings)

39. About Jack Lookman

Olayinka Carew, aka Jack Lookman is the 1st of 5 Children.
He has 3 children, and an elderly mum. He is resident in the United Kingdom and is of Nigerian origin.

He studied at King's College, Lagos and University of Lagos.
He has varied life and work experiences.
He has been involved in voluntary and paid jobs.
He is dedicating the rest of his life to empowering and inspiring generations.
This is one of his legacy projects.
Though he has health challenges, he does not let that impede his mission and vision.
Even though he studied Engineering in University; his calling is so many miles away from that. He is currently an Entrepreneur, Content Creator, Affiliate Marketer and Mentor.

He is the Director and Owner of Jack Lookman Limited, a registered business in the United Kingdom; and their aim is to empower and inspire generations by leveraging the internet.

jacksempowerment.com.   jacklookman.co.uk.   jaaloo.com

40. OTHER PUBLICATIONS BY JACK LOOKMAN LIMITED

1. Despair, Submission, Faith and Hope – Volume 1
2. Despair, Submission, Faith and Hope – Volume 2
3. Monetising Digital Book Reviews
4. E-Commerce For Traditional African Attires
5. Basic Management And Fundraising Tip For Community Groups
6. Monetising A Digital Library
7. Ajo, The App And Opportunities
8. Empowering Orphans, Widows and Widowers
9. Submission, Gratitude, Faith and Hope
10. Oro Ishiti- Indelible Yoruba Words
11. Eid Monetisation by Leveraging Technology
12. What are your thoughts? What is your mindset? - Volume 1
13. What are your thoughts? What is your mindset? - Volume 2
14. Twenty Curated Business Ideas - Volume 1
15. Jaaloo Puzzles - Volume 1
16. Jaaloo Puzzles - Volume 2
17. Beauty Of The Storm
18. Digital Career Guidance App
19. Bath Sponge Project
20. Community Group Monetisation
21. Profit Sharing Formula App

22. Event Discount App

23. Leasing Digital Tablets / Gadgets To Undergraduates

24. Monetising Jollof Rice

jacksempowerment.com.   jacklookman.co.uk.   jaaloo.com

41. Some Useful Links

Blog: jacklookman.co.uk

Membership Site: jacksempowerment.com

Game: jaaloo.com

Jack Lookman's Books: https://www.amazon.co.uk/s?k=jack+lookman&crid=2LD8LZ1UP7VS6&sprefix=,aps,46&ref=nb_sb_ss_recent_1_0_recent

Or visit amazon.co.uk search for Jack Lookman

Ebooks: https://selar.co/m/jacklookman

Youtube channel: Jack Lookman: https://youtube.com/@jacklookman

Youtube channel: Business Ideas etc: https://youtube.com/@businessideasetc5620

Facebook: https://www.facebook.com/jack.lookman.3

Facebook group: Business Ideas etc: https://www.facebook.com/groups/353168765939448/?ref=share_group_link

Facebook group: Jack's Affiliate Marketing Academy: https://www.facebook.com/groups/jaclookman/?ref=share_group_link

Complementary video: https://youtu.be/UULsprbNQRw

Why you shouldn't celebrate your birthday: https://selar.co/WYSCYB

Jack The Mentor - Mentoring And Coaching: https://www.jacksempowerment.com/products/courses/view/1139388

Jack's Mentoring 101: https://www.jacksempowerment.com/products/courses/view/1152633